Reader's Journal
for the
United States Catholic Catechism
for Adults

AD HOC COMMITTEE TO OVERSEE THE USE OF THE *CATECHISM*

United States Conference of Catholic Bishops
Washington, D.C.

The *Reader's Journal for the United States Catholic Catechism for Adults* was developed as a resource by the Ad Hoc Committee to Oversee the Use of the *Catechism* of the United States Conference of Catholic Bishops (USCCB). It was reviewed by the committee chairman, Archbishop Alfred C. Hughes, and has been authorized for publication by the undersigned.

Msgr. David J. Malloy
General Secretary, USCCB

First Printing, September 2007

ISBN 978-1-60137-003-7

CONTENTS

Part 3: Christian Morality: The Faith Lived

Part 4: Prayer: The Faith Prayed

INTRODUCTION

"From the earliest days of the Church when St. Athanasius wrote the life of St. Anthony of the Desert, it was clear that telling stories about saints and holy people encourages others to want to be like them and is an effective way of teaching Catholic doctrine."

—United States Catholic Catechism for Adults, xx

In this *Reader's Journal for the United States Catholic Catechism for Adults*, the starting point is your personal response to the teachings of the Catholic faith revealed to us in and through Christ Jesus, the Lord. As in the stories of faith that begin each chapter of the *United States Catholic Catechism for Adults* (USCCA), the connection between Catholic teaching and Catholic living lies in the unfolding story of each one of our lives.

The thirty-six chapters in this *Reader's Journal* parallel the thirty-six chapters of the USCCA. For selected sections of each chapter, you will find reflection questions and space to respond with your thoughts and insights. Each chapter in this journal ends with the challenge to identify how to put your faith into practice.

This *Reader's Journal* provides rich opportunities to articulate your faith and to reflect on how to live that faith in new and deeper ways.

WHO SHOULD USE THIS READER'S JOURNAL?

- **Individuals:** Use this *Reader's Journal* by focusing on each chapter for a specific period of time, such as a week or a month. During this time, read and reflect on sections of the corresponding USCCA chapter, and respond in the journal at regular intervals as your schedule allows. While reading each chapter, use the prayer suggestions daily, and reflect regularly on ways to live out your faith.

- **RCIA:** The *Reader's Journal* is a perfect resource for catechumens, the elect, and candidates for reception into full communion. The journal will aid both their catechesis and their mystagogical reflection. When the section of the chapter being studied has a reflection step in the journal, invite participants to write down their personal reflections and responses before sharing with the group. This activity provides an opportunity for the insights of individuals to enrich the group as a whole.

- **Adult Faith Formation Groups:** Anyone participating in adult faith formation efforts in the parish can use this *Reader's Journal* for additional reflection after scheduled sessions. Small groups can use it to facilitate reflection and discussion. Individuals within the parish can establish a parish message board or blog online for parishioners to share their reflections throughout the year.

This *Reader's Journal for the United States Catholic Catechism for Adults* will provide many opportunities for individuals and groups to grow in knowing, understanding, and living the Catholic faith.

HOW DO I USE THIS READER'S JOURNAL?

- This *Reader's Journal* is a companion to the *United States Catholic Catechism for Adults* (USCCA). Refer to the USCCA often as you reflect on the questions in this journal.

- Begin using this *Reader's Journal* by asking God to open your heart and mind to the Church teaching found in the corresponding USCCA chapter. Ask God to help you discern how that teaching can support and strengthen your life of faith by leading you to a closer relationship with the Holy Trinity: Father, Son, and Holy Spirit.

- Determine how you will schedule regular progress through the journal, whether by week, month, or other specific period of time:

  — You could focus on a USCCA chapter each week. Challenge yourself to read and reflect on each section of the chapter. Make it a daily habit to follow one of the prayer suggestions in this *Reader's Journal* for that week. Consider how the teaching in each week's chapter invites you to live your faith more fully.

  — Or work through a chapter or two per month. Use a phrase from one of the prayers or the meditation as a daily mantra as you travel to work, care for your family, run errands, or do chores. In the last week of each month, focus on living your faith more deeply and with greater intentionality.

- Use each section in the *Reader's Journal* to pause in your reading of the USCCA, reflect on what you have read, and respond by recording your insights, reactions, and even questions. Your written responses will help you create a record of yourself at a particular time and place in your journey of faith. Feel free to use the pages at the end of this book or a separate notebook if additional space is needed.

- Use the sections in the back of the USCCA to help you grow in your knowledge and love of the faith:

  — *Appendix A: Glossary.* This glossary will help you become fluent in the language of the Catholic faith and offers basic definitions of terms that may be unfamiliar.

  — *Appendix B: Traditional Catholic Prayers.* This collection includes prayers that you may wish to memorize so that they become part of your regular prayer life. This appendix also includes directions for praying the Rosary.

  — *Appendix C: For Further Reading.* This appendix points you to other documents of the Church that will help you learn more about the teachings introduced in the USCCA.

  — *Scriptural Index.* The USCCA includes numerous references to the Bible. This index includes all those references to help you see the essential role of the Word of God in Church teaching. Use this index to identify Scripture passages for further reading and reflection.

  — *Index.* When reading, reflecting, or responding requires further clarification or definition, the index will direct you to the appropriate page(s) in the USCCA and to relevant definitions in the glossary.

This *Reader's Journal for the United States Catholic Catechism for Adults* was developed to help you make the USCCA part of your

ABBREVIATIONS IN THIS JOURNAL

CCC   *Catechism of the Catholic Church*, 2nd ed. (Washington, DC: United States Conference of Catholic Bishops, 2000).

RCIA   Rite of Christian Initiation of Adults.

USCCA   *United States Catholic Catechism for Adults* (Washington, DC: United States Conference of Catholic Bishops, 2006).

Other abbreviations, including books of the Bible, may be found on pages xiii-xiv of the USCCA.

faith journey. Using this journal offers unique opportunities to learn the teachings of the Church and to recognize their implications for your life, whether you are a baptized member of the Catholic Church or someone seeking Baptism or reception into the Catholic Church.

This *Reader's Journal* will be a beneficial aid on your journey of faith. The Catholic teaching you learn, the moments of prayer you experience, and the many ways in which you allow your learning to penetrate the way you live—all will guide you into a life rooted in Jesus Christ, drawing you closer to our heavenly Father through the action of the Holy Spirit. May you ultimately come to share in the life of the Holy Trinity!

PART I

THE CREED:
THE FAITH PROFESSED

1 MY SOUL LONGS FOR YOU, O GOD (Ps 42:2)

THE HUMAN QUEST FOR GOD
—CCC, NOS. 27-43

——— READ • REFLECT • RESPOND ———

ONE WOMAN'S QUEST
PAGES 1-3

The story of St. Elizabeth Ann Seton highlights how she responded to her longing to know God and to draw closer to him. How can her example inspire you in your faith journey?

THROUGH CREATION
PAGES 3-4

When has a personal experience of the beauty and power of the created world affirmed the existence of God for you?

A GENERATION OF SEEKERS
PAGES 6-7

Describe a person or place that helps you experience God's presence.

FOR DISCUSSION
PAGE 7

Read the Discussion Questions in this chapter and use the space below to respond to those for which you have an immediate answer. Later, return to the questions you found more challenging, and invite the Holy Spirit to guide you in responding.

DOCTRINAL STATEMENTS
PAGES 7-8

Read the doctrinal statements for Chapter 1. They will help you to focus on the particular content of the chapter. Record in this journal any insights from reading this summary of the chapter's teaching.

MEDITATION
PAGE 8

Slowly and reflectively read the Meditation for Chapter 1. Select a word or phrase that is especially meaningful, and spend time thinking of its significance for your life. Record the word or phrase below, and reflect on it often, even daily.

SUGGESTIONS FOR PRAYER
PAGE 9

As you began this chapter by reading Psalm 42:2, now conclude by reading Psalm 42:2-6. Include this psalm in your daily prayer.

Turn to the Prayer to the Holy Spirit in USCCA Appendix B, page 534. Pray it in thanksgiving to the Holy Spirit for being with you as you reflected and responded to the teaching in Chapter 1.

PUTTING FAITH INTO PRACTICE

This week, as a result of reading, reflecting, and responding to Chapter 1, I am inspired to . . .

2 GOD COMES TO MEET US

GOD REVEALS A PLAN OF LOVING GOODNESS
—CCC, NOS. 50-67

READ • REFLECT • RESPOND

GOD REVEALS HIS HOLY NAME
PAGES 11-12

In revealing himself to us, God wants us to respond to him, to know him, and to love him. How do you see God revealing himself to you each day? How do you respond to God?

GOD'S LOVING PLAN TO SAVE US
PAGES 12-15

Through his revealing word and divine action, God seeks an intimate relationship with you. How does it feel to know this? What does it mean to have an intimate relationship with God?

THE GOSPEL AND CULTURE
PAGES 15-17

Think of a time when you were pressured to disregard or deny your religious beliefs. How did you feel? How did you respond?

FOR DISCUSSION
PAGE 17

Read the Discussion Questions in this chapter and use the space below to respond to those for which you have an immediate answer. Later, return to the questions you found more challenging, and invite the Holy Spirit to guide you in responding.

DOCTRINAL STATEMENTS
PAGES 17-18

Read the doctrinal statements for Chapter 2. They will help you to focus on the particular content of the chapter. Record in this journal any insights from reading this summary of the chapter's teaching.

MEDITATE • PRAY • ACT

MEDITATION
PAGE 18

Slowly and reflectively read the Meditation for Chapter 2. Select a word or phrase that is especially meaningful, and spend time thinking of its significance for your life. Record the word or phrase below, and reflect on it often, even daily.

SUGGESTIONS FOR PRAYER
PAGE 19

Read the closing prayer, Psalm 119:89-90, 105. Include this psalm in your daily prayer.

How can you work to "supplement your faith with virtue," as St. Peter advocates (2 Pt 1:5)?

PUTTING FAITH INTO PRACTICE

This week, as a result of reading, reflecting, and responding to Chapter 2, I am inspired to . . .

3 PROCLAIM THE GOSPEL TO EVERY CREATURE (Mk 16:15)

THE TRANSMISSION OF DIVINE REVELATION
—CCC, NOS. 74-133

─────── READ • REFLECT • RESPOND ───────

HANDING ON THE FAITH
PAGES 21-23

Empowered by the leadership of Blessed John XXIII, the Church asked herself how to better communicate doctrine or the Church's teaching to the men and women of the twentieth century. How can the USCCA help you understand your beliefs more clearly? How can the USCCA help you share your beliefs with others?

SACRED TRADITION
PAGES 23-26

Think of a time when you realized that your beliefs have come to you from Jesus Christ through his Church. How did that realization bring you closer to Christ, the founder and head of the Church?

SACRED SCRIPTURE
PAGES 26-27

How does knowing that God is the author of Sacred Scripture deepen your appreciation of the Bible? How does understanding the literal and spiritual senses of Scripture enhance your reading of the Bible?

OTHER BIBLICAL INTERPRETATIONS
PAGES 28-31

Many people believe only in the Bible, whereas the Catholic Church accepts that both Scripture and Tradition, the Deposit of Faith, reveal God to us. How can this teaching strengthen your confidence in the beliefs and traditions of your faith?

FOR DISCUSSION
PAGE 31

Read the Discussion Questions in this chapter and use the space below to respond to those for which you have an immediate answer. Later, return to the questions you found more challenging, and invite the Holy Spirit to guide you in responding.

DOCTRINAL STATEMENTS
PAGES 31-32

Read the doctrinal statements for Chapter 3. They will help you to focus on the particular content of the chapter. Record in this journal any insights from reading this summary of the chapter's teaching.

MEDITATE • PRAY • ACT

MEDITATION
PAGES 32-33

Slowly and reflectively read the Meditation for Chapter 3. Select a word or phrase that is especially meaningful, and spend time thinking of its significance for your life. Record the word or phrase below, and reflect on it often, even daily.

SUGGESTIONS FOR PRAYER
PAGE 33

Read the prayer of St. Augustine and the advice from Paul's second letter to the Thessalonians. From either, record a line in this journal to recite each time you open your Bible.

PUTTING FAITH INTO PRACTICE

This week, as a result of reading, reflecting, and responding to Chapter 3, I am inspired to . . .

4 BRING ABOUT THE OBEDIENCE OF FAITH

FAITH AS THE HUMAN RESPONSE TO GOD'S REVELATION
—CCC, NOS. 142-197

———— READ • REFLECT • RESPOND ————

MISSIONARY TO THE AMERICAN PEOPLE
PAGES 35-37

We may not be gifted with the eloquence of Isaac Hecker. Yet we are called, as disciples of Jesus Christ, to share our faith with others. How do you respond to this call?

RESPOND TO GOD'S REVELATION
PAGES 36-37

Through an utterly free decision, God has revealed and given himself to us so that we may respond to him, know him, and love him. Describe a time when you were aware that God was revealing himself to you in a person, place, or event.

BELIEVE IN THE LORD JESUS
PAGES 37-39

Review the six qualities of faith listed on these two pages. Which one speaks to you, and why?

THE FAITH PILGRIMAGE
PAGES 39-41

Just as God's Revelation of himself to us is gradual, so too is our response. Think of a specific, meaningful moment in your faith journey. Why was that moment so significant?

CHALLENGES TO FAITH
PAGES 41-43

When do your Catholic beliefs and identity place you in opposition to the values of your culture?

FOR DISCUSSION
PAGE 44

Read the Discussion Questions in this chapter and use the space below to respond to those for which you have an immediate answer. Later, return to the questions you found more challenging, and invite the Holy Spirit to guide you in responding.

DOCTRINAL STATEMENTS
PAGES 44-45

Read the doctrinal statements for Chapter 4. They will help you to focus on the particular content of the chapter. Record in this journal any insights from reading this summary of the chapter's teaching.

———— MEDITATE • PRAY • ACT ————

MEDITATION
PAGE 45

Slowly and reflectively read the Meditation for Chapter 4. Select a word or phrase that is especially meaningful, and spend time thinking of its significance for your life. Record the word or phrase below, and reflect on it often, even daily.

SUGGESTIONS FOR PRAYER
PAGES 45-47

We recite the Nicene Creed during the Mass each Sunday and on special feasts, but the Apostles' Creed provides the basis for the renewal of our baptismal promises at Easter and is recited each time we pray the Rosary. How can you include the Apostles' Creed more frequently in your prayer life?

PUTTING FAITH INTO PRACTICE

This week, as a result of reading, reflecting, and responding to Chapter 4, I am inspired to . . .

5 I BELIEVE IN GOD

FAITH IN GOD AS MYSTERY AND TRINITY;
BELIEF IN GOD, THE FATHER ALMIGHTY,
CREATOR OF HEAVEN AND EARTH
—CCC, NOS. 199-349

READ • REFLECT • RESPOND

AN INTELLECTUAL CATHOLIC
PAGES 49-50

Orestes Brownson, a great thinker and intellectual, relied on the teaching authority of the Church to provide a map for his faith journey. How do you firmly root your life in the teachings of the Church?

HOLY MYSTERY
PAGES 50-51

How does your knowledge of God mature as you mature?

THE TRINITY
PAGES 51-53

The mystery of the Trinity is the central mystery of the Christian faith. What does this mystery mean at this point in your faith journey? What questions do you have about this mystery?

CREATOR OF HEAVEN AND EARTH
PAGES 53-54

God created heaven and earth, "all that is seen and unseen." How do you show reverence for yourself as one of God's creations?

THE ANGELS
PAGES 54-55

Angels have resurfaced in popular culture; for example, many people wear "angel pins." Yet the angels are far more than our culture realizes. How does this section inform, change, or strengthen your belief in angels?

DIVINE PROVIDENCE
PAGE 56

The *Catechism of the Catholic Church* teaches that "God cares for all, from the least things to the great events of the world and its history" (no. 303). How can you abandon yourself to the will of God for your life?

THE REALITY OF EVIL
PAGES 56-57

We are reminded every day that there is evil in our world. Yet even the smallest act of goodness is effective against evil. How can you, as a disciple of Jesus Christ, displace evil with good?

ISSUES OF FAITH AND SCIENCE

Our society constantly searches for answers and relies on science to explain the mysteries of life. How can the Church's moral teachings guide you when scientific research does not reflect those teachings?

FOR DISCUSSION
PAGE 61

Read the Discussion Questions in this chapter and use the space below to respond to those for which you have an immediate answer. Later, return to the questions you found more challenging, and invite the Holy Spirit to guide you in responding.

DOCTRINAL STATEMENTS
PAGES 61-62

Read the doctrinal statements for Chapter 5. They will help you to focus on the particular content of the chapter. Record in this journal any insights from reading this summary of the chapter's teaching.

───── MEDITATE • PRAY • ACT ─────

MEDITATION
PAGE 63

Slowly and reflectively read the Meditation for Chapter 5. Select a word or phrase that is especially meaningful, and spend time thinking of its significance for your life. Record the word or phrase below, and reflect on it often, even daily.

SUGGESTIONS FOR PRAYER
PAGE 63

The Act of Faith is a traditional Catholic prayer that you may wish to memorize. When you are asked what you believe, this prayer gives you a condensed answer. Pray this prayer and ask the Holy Spirit to increase your faith.

PUTTING FAITH INTO PRACTICE

This week, as a result of reading, reflecting, and responding to Chapter 5, I am inspired to . . .

6 MAN AND WOMAN IN THE BEGINNING

THE CREATION OF MAN AND WOMAN,
THE FALL AND THE PROMISE
—CCC, NOS. 355-421

READ • REFLECT • RESPOND

THE HOUSE OF MERCY
PAGES 65-67

Many of us have loved ones who suffer from physical, emotional, or mental illness. In what way, however small, can you imitate the example of Rose Hawthorne?

CREATED IN GOD'S IMAGE
PAGES 67-68

We are created in the image and likeness of God and have received the gift of free will. How do you allow God's grace to help you conform your will to his?

THE FALL
PAGES 68-69

Why is it that, with the best of intentions, we find it so difficult to do what is right?

THE IMPACT OF ORIGINAL SIN
PAGES 69-70

By Baptism we are freed from Original Sin and all personal sins and are turned back to God. What does it mean to you that you are born again in this sacrament?

UNDERSTANDING SIN
PAGES 71-72

How can you acknowledge Jesus as the one who is responsible for your salvation? How does this chapter help you to pray even more fervently the words of the Lord's Prayer: "deliver us from evil"?

FOR DISCUSSION
PAGES 72-73

Read the Discussion Questions in this chapter and use the space below to respond to those for which you have an immediate answer. Later, return to the questions you found more challenging, and invite the Holy Spirit to guide you in responding.

DOCTRINAL STATEMENTS
PAGES 73-74

Read the doctrinal statements for Chapter 6. They will help you to focus on the particular content of the chapter. Record in this journal any insights from reading this summary of the chapter's teaching.

———— MEDITATE • PRAY • ACT ————

MEDITATION
PAGES 74-75

Slowly and reflectively read the Meditation for Chapter 6. Select a word or phrase that is especially meaningful, and spend time thinking of its significance for your life. Record the word or phrase below, and reflect on it often, even daily.

SUGGESTIONS FOR PRAYER
PAGE 75

As you read the words of Rose Hawthorne Lathrop, consider the opportunities you have to practice your faith each day. Thank God, who is all good, for placing in your heart the desire to think, speak, and do good.

PUTTING FAITH INTO PRACTICE

This week, as a result of reading, reflecting, and responding to Chapter 6, I am inspired to . . .

7 THE GOOD NEWS: GOD HAS SENT HIS SON

SON OF GOD, SON OF MARY,
MYSTERIES OF CHRIST'S LIFE
—CCC, NOS. 422-570

—— READ • REFLECT • RESPOND ——

A GOOD MAN IN OLD NEW YORK
PAGES 77-79

Venerable Pierre Toussaint was an incredibly generous and loving man. His motivation was his profound love of Jesus Christ. While you may not be able to alleviate others' sufferings exactly as he did, how can you imitate him, especially through the social outreach programs of your parish?

GOSPEL PORTRAITS OF JESUS
PAGES 79-80

If we want to know Jesus, we should know the Scripture. How, when, and where can you begin reading the New Testament daily, in order to know Jesus better?

TRUE GOD AND TRUE MAN
PAGES 81-83

Jesus is fully God and fully man. As a man, he was like you in all things except sin. For our sake, he suffered, died, and rose from the dead. How does all this help you relate to him?

JESUS IS THE SAVIOR OF ALL
PAGES 84-85

How can knowing of Jesus' love for all challenge your attitude and actions toward others, regardless of differences?

FOR DISCUSSION
PAGE 85

Read the Discussion Questions in this chapter and use the space below to respond to those for which you have an immediate answer. Later, return to the questions you found more challenging, and invite the Holy Spirit to guide you in responding.

DOCTRINAL STATEMENTS
PAGES 85-86

Read the doctrinal statements for Chapter 7. They will help you to focus on the particular content of the chapter. Record in this journal any insights from reading this summary of the chapter's teaching.

───────── MEDITATE • PRAY • ACT ─────────

MEDITATION
PAGES 86-87

Slowly and reflectively read the Meditation for Chapter 7. Select a word or phrase that is especially meaningful, and spend time thinking of its significance for your life. Record the word or phrase below, and reflect on it often, even daily.

SUGGESTIONS FOR PRAYER
PAGE 87

Develop the good habit of a nightly examination of conscience, in which you review and reflect on the day. At this time, say the prayer at the end of this chapter, asking God for his mercy.

PUTTING FAITH INTO PRACTICE

This week, as a result of reading, reflecting, and responding to Chapter 7, I am inspired to . . .

8 THE SAVING DEATH AND RESURRECTION OF CHRIST

THE PASCHAL MYSTERY, UNITY OF THE SAVING DEEDS
—CCC, NOS. 571-664

———— READ • REFLECT • RESPOND ————

SINGING THE LORD'S PRAISES
PAGES 89-90

Through good health as well as years of suffering, the social conscience of Sr. Thea Bowman characterized her presence in the Church in the United States. How can you serve the needs of others, especially those who are suffering?

LIFT HIGH THE CROSS
PAGES 91-93

Have you ever been insulted? Hurt? Wounded in some way? How can you, in imitation of Christ, forgive those responsible? If you have forgiven them, how did you do so?

CHRIST IS RISEN! ALLELUIA!
PAGES 93-94

Our attitude towards death reflects our Christian belief that death is not the end. How can this belief lessen your fear of death? How can you live in greater awareness of the possibility of heaven and union with God?

HISTORICAL EVENT
PAGES 94-95

Mary Magdalene, the Apostles, and the disciples on the road to Emmaus were witnesses to the Resurrection of Jesus Christ. You live in a culture that says "seeing is believing." Yet in John 20:29, Jesus tells us, "Blessed are those who have not seen and have believed." How does your faith help you to understand the words of Jesus?

A TRANSCENDENT EVENT
PAGE 95

In this section you read, "If Jesus had not risen, our faith would mean nothing." How do you explain the meaning of these words?

THE ASCENSION INTO HEAVEN
PAGES 96-97

At the Ascension, Jesus' humanity entered into divine glory and opened the possibility that we also may go where he is. How often do you think about heaven? How does the promise of heaven affect how you live your life?

FROM DOUBT TO FAITH
PAGES 97-98

Have you had doubts about the Resurrection of Jesus Christ and its significance for your salvation? How did you come to believe in the Resurrection? How has that belief grown stronger in your adulthood?

FOR DISCUSSION
PAGE 98

Read the Discussion Questions in this chapter and use the space below to respond to those for which you have an immediate answer. Later, return to the questions you found more challenging, and invite the Holy Spirit to guide you in responding.

DOCTRINAL STATEMENTS

PAGES 98-99

Read the doctrinal statements for Chapter 8. They will help you to focus on the particular content of the chapter. Record in this journal any insights from reading this summary of the chapter's teaching.

——————— MEDITATE • PRAY • ACT ———————

MEDITATION

PAGE 99

Slowly and reflectively read the Meditation for Chapter 8. Select a word or phrase that is especially meaningful, and spend time thinking of its significance for your life. Record the word or phrase below, and reflect on it often, even daily.

SUGGESTIONS FOR PRAYER

PAGE 100

This Byzantine hymn invites you to "always bless the Lord." Seize every opportunity to praise God for sending his Son, Jesus Christ, to save you and give you the promise of eternal life.

PUTTING FAITH INTO PRACTICE

This week, as a result of reading, reflecting, and responding to Chapter 8, I am inspired to . . .

9 RECEIVE THE HOLY SPIRIT (Jn 20:22)

THE REVELATION OF THE SPIRIT,
JOINT MISSION OF SON AND SPIRIT
—CCC, NOS. 683-747

———— READ • REFLECT • RESPOND ————

SHE WAS LED BY THE HOLY SPIRIT
PAGES 101-102

Have you ever been challenged, criticized, or mocked for your faith? How has the Holy Spirit helped you to defend your faith?

THE TRANSFORMING SPIRIT
PAGES 102-104

The Holy Spirit first comes to us in the Sacrament of Baptism. How do you rely upon the Holy Spirit to live your faith? How do you witness to your faith as a family member? As a Catholic? As a neighbor?

THE HOLY SPIRIT IS REVEALED GRADUALLY
PAGES 104-106

This section describes the eight ways in which the Holy Spirit is present in your life. Which of these eight have you experienced, and how?

FOR DISCUSSION
PAGE 108

Read the Discussion Questions in this chapter and use the space below to respond to those for which you have an immediate answer. Later, return to the questions you found more challenging, and invite the Holy Spirit to guide you in responding.

DOCTRINAL STATEMENTS
PAGES 108-109

Read the doctrinal statements for Chapter 9. They will help you to focus on the particular content of the chapter. Record in this journal any insights from reading this summary of the chapter's teaching.

MEDITATE • PRAY • ACT

MEDITATION
PAGES 109-110

Slowly and reflectively read the Meditation for Chapter 9. Select a word or phrase that is especially meaningful, and spend time thinking of its significance for your life. Record the word or phrase below, and reflect on it often, even daily.

SUGGESTIONS FOR PRAYER
PAGE 110

Make this prayer to the Holy Spirit part of your prayer life. Pray the words "Come, Holy Spirit" before opening the USCCA. Pray these words whenever you read, reflect, and respond to this journal.

PUTTING FAITH INTO PRACTICE

This week, as a result of reading, reflecting, and responding to Chapter 9, I am inspired to . . .

10 THE CHURCH: REFLECTING THE LIGHT OF CHRIST

IMAGES AND MISSION OF THE CHURCH
—CCC, NOS. 748-810

—————— READ • REFLECT • RESPOND ——————

A ROCK AND A LOVING PASTOR
PAGES 111-112

How does your faith help you believe in Jesus as the Second Person of the Trinity? As your Savior? As founder and head of the Catholic Church?

THE CHURCH AS MYSTERY
PAGES 112-113

The Church, empowered by the Holy Spirit, is the instrument of your salvation. How has the Church helped you to grow in holiness?

THE WORD "CHURCH"
PAGE 113

The Second Vatican Council called the home the "domestic Church." How do you maintain your home as a "domestic Church"?

PLANNED BY THE FATHER
PAGE 113

God has invited all persons to enter into a relationship with him. How does the Church help you to respond to God's invitation?

FOUNDED BY JESUS CHRIST
PAGE 114

How do you feel when you recognize that the Catholic Church was founded by Jesus Christ, the Son of God? In what way does the Church show forth its divine foundation?

REVEALED BY THE SPIRIT
PAGES 114-115

How do you feel when you realize that the Holy Spirit has been, remains, and will always be with the Church through all circumstances?

THE SACRAMENT OF SALVATION
PAGES 115-116

The Church is one, and the Holy Spirit is the source of that oneness. How do you experience the *visible* reality of the Church? How do you experience the *spiritual* reality of the Church?

A PRIESTLY PEOPLE

PAGE 117

Catholics sometimes say that they are "offering up" something. Everything we do can be a spiritual offering when united to Christ's sacrifice. Do you use this expression? How does this section help you understand it?

A PROPHETIC PEOPLE

PAGES 117-118

Have you ever said, "Actions speak louder than words"? How does this section affirm the truth of this saying?

A ROYAL PEOPLE

PAGE 118

By Baptism, we share in the royal office of Jesus Christ. Reflect on the explanation of servant leadership found in this section. How do you carry out this role? In what new ways can you lead through loving service?

UPON THIS ROCK

PAGES 119-121

How does your parish serve the needs of its members? Of the community? Of the larger Church?

FOR DISCUSSION
PAGE 121

Read the Discussion Questions in this chapter and use the space below to respond to those for which you have an immediate answer. Later, return to the questions you found more challenging, and invite the Holy Spirit to guide you in responding.

DOCTRINAL STATEMENTS
PAGE 122

Read the doctrinal statements for Chapter 10. They will help you to focus on the particular content of the chapter. Record in this journal any insights from reading this summary of the chapter's teaching.

MEDITATE • PRAY • ACT

MEDITATION
PAGE 123

Slowly and reflectively read the Meditation for Chapter 10. Select a word or phrase that is especially meaningful, and spend time thinking of its significance for your life. Record the word or phrase below, and reflect on it often, even daily.

SUGGESTIONS FOR PRAYER
PAGE 123

The prayers at the end of this chapter highlight how much God exalts us by calling us to be his own people, members of his Church. Pray that the Church may ever be all that God has called her to be.

PUTTING FAITH INTO PRACTICE

This week, as a result of reading, reflecting, and responding to Chapter 10, I am inspired to . . .

11 THE FOUR MARKS OF THE CHURCH

THE CHURCH IS ONE, HOLY, CATHOLIC, AND APOSTOLIC
—CCC, NOS. 811-962

READ • REFLECT • RESPOND

I WANTED TO BE A MISSIONARY
PAGES 125-126

Christ said to his Apostles, "Go, therefore, and make disciples of all nations" (Mt 28:19). How do you respond to this mandate?

THE CHURCH IS ONE
PAGES 127-129

When members of a family do not share a common religion, they can experience real friction. If this is true of your family, how do you handle your differences? How are you a healing presence in your family?

THE CHURCH IS HOLY
PAGE 129

Each of us is a sinner, yet we are called to be holy. How do you respond to that call? How do you contribute to the holiness of your loved ones? How do you make your home a place where your family can become holy?

THE CHURCH IS CATHOLIC
PAGES 129-131

Through our daily lives and the media, we encounter the great diversity in the world community. That diversity can also be found in our families, our neighborhoods, our parishes. How do you experience the world's diversity? What is your attitude towards diversity?

THE CHURCH IS APOSTOLIC
PAGES 132-134

Christ built his Church on the Apostles. Today the pope and the bishops are the successors of the Apostles. Who is the pope, the head of the Catholic Church? Who are your bishop(s) and your pastor(s)? Why is it important to know this information?

LAITY
PAGES 134-135

How do you currently volunteer in your parish? If you do not, who can you talk to about using your gifts for the good of your parish?

CONSECRATED LIFE
PAGE 135

The Church encourages its members to pray for vocations to the consecrated life. What is your attitude towards young men and women considering the consecrated life as their vocation in life? How can you foster vocations?

MAKE DISCIPLES
PAGES 135-137

Read Fr. Alvin Illig's thoughts on six ways in which everyone can evangelize. Which way seems like a realistic first step for you to become an evangelizing person? Identify a second step, third step, etc.

FOR DISCUSSION
PAGE 137

Read the Discussion Questions in this chapter and use the space below to respond to those for which you have an immediate answer. Later, return to the questions you found more challenging, and invite the Holy Spirit to guide you in responding.

DOCTRINAL STATEMENTS
PAGES 138-139

Read the doctrinal statements for Chapter 11. They will help you to focus on the particular content of the chapter. Record in this journal any insights from reading this summary of the chapter's teaching.

———————— MEDITATE • PRAY • ACT ————————

MEDITATION
PAGE 139

Slowly and reflectively read the Meditation for Chapter 11. Select a word or phrase that is especially meaningful, and spend time thinking of its significance for your life. Record the word or phrase below, and reflect on it often, even daily.

SUGGESTIONS FOR PRAYER
PAGE 139

The Intercessions from the Common of the Apostles remind us that sins committed after Baptism can be forgiven. During your busy life, carve out time to celebrate the Sacraments of Penance and the Eucharist in order to restore the communion with God that is lost through sin.

PUTTING FAITH INTO PRACTICE

This week, as a result of reading, reflecting, and responding to Chapter 11, I am inspired to . . .

12 MARY: THE CHURCH'S FIRST AND MOST PERFECT MEMBER

MARY, MOTHER OF JESUS, MOTHER OF GOD,
MOTHER OF THE CHURCH
—CCC, NOS. 484-507, 963-972, 2673-2677

READ • REFLECT • RESPOND

ST. JUAN DIEGO SEES MARY
PAGES 141-143

Pilgrims are drawn to places where Mary has appeared. But we do not have to go to Guadalupe, Fatima, or Lourdes to pray to Mary and ask her to intercede with God. How do you make Mary part of your prayer life?

GOD'S PLAN FOR MARY
PAGE 143

The Gospels paint a picture of Mary for us. What inspires you about Mary or her life?

BLESSED ARE YOU AMONG WOMEN
PAGES 143-146

Mary said "yes" to God when asked to be the Mother of his Son. How can Mary's "yes" inspire you to accept the will of God in your life?

MARY AS MOTHER OF THE CHURCH
PAGE 146

You are a member of the Church, and Mary is the Mother of the Church. What helps you to accept Mary as your Mother?

MARY'S MATERNAL INTERCESSION
PAGES 146-147

How do you seek Mary's prayer and help for yourself? For your family? For others for whom you care or worry?

FOR DISCUSSION
PAGE 147

Read the Discussion Questions in this chapter and use the space below to respond to those for which you have an immediate answer. Later, return to the questions you found more challenging, and invite the Holy Spirit to guide you in responding.

DOCTRINAL STATEMENTS
PAGES 147-148

Read the doctrinal statements for Chapter 12. They will help you to focus on the particular content of the chapter. Record in this journal any insights from reading this summary of the chapter's teaching.

———— MEDITATE • PRAY • ACT ————

MEDITATION
PAGES 148-149

Slowly and reflectively read the Meditation for Chapter 12. Select a word or phrase that is especially meaningful, and spend time thinking of its significance for your life. Record the word or phrase below, and reflect on it often, even daily.

SUGGESTIONS FOR PRAYER
PAGE 149

The *Memorare* is a prayer that many Catholics commit to memory. If you have not done so already, make this prayer your own.

PUTTING FAITH INTO PRACTICE

This week, as a result of reading, reflecting, and responding to Chapter 12, I am inspired to . . .

13 OUR ETERNAL DESTINY

LAST THINGS: RESURRECTION OF THE BODY,
DEATH, PARTICULAR JUDGMENT, HEAVEN,
PURGATORY, HELL, LAST JUDGMENT,
NEW HEAVENS, AND NEW EARTH
—CCC, NOS. 988-1065

——— READ • REFLECT • RESPOND ———

LOVE IS PROVED BY DEEDS
PAGES 151-152

St. Katharine Drexel focused on the teaching of the Gospel, so that those she served might have full life here on earth and the ultimate fullness of life in heaven. Each day, what can you do to make your earthly life more meaningful? What can you do each day to prepare for the life to come?

THE MEANING OF CHRISTIAN DEATH
PAGES 153-155

At the end of our days on earth, we will be judged according to how we loved God, others, and ourselves. How can you grow in this love?

THE RESURRECTION OF THE BODY
PAGES 155-156

Catholics believe in the resurrection of the body on Judgment Day. How does this teaching affect your life of faith?

THE LAST JUDGMENT
PAGES 156-157

One day we will be judged and either inherit the Kingdom of God or not. How does this teaching affect the way you live today?

CHRISTIAN DEATH
PAGES 158-159

Too often today, the aging, the sick, and the dying are abandoned. How does your parish serve the needs of these people? Who coordinates these efforts? How can you get involved?

FOR DISCUSSION
PAGE 160

Read the Discussion Questions in this chapter and use the space below to respond to those for which you have an immediate answer. Later, return to the questions you found more challenging, and invite the Holy Spirit to guide you in responding.

DOCTRINAL STATEMENTS
PAGES 160-161

Read the doctrinal statements for Chapter 13. They will help you to focus on the particular content of the chapter. Record in this journal any insights from reading this summary of the chapter's teaching.

———————— MEDITATE • PRAY • ACT ————————

MEDITATION
PAGE 162

Slowly and reflectively read the Meditation for Chapter 13. Select a word or phrase that is especially meaningful, and spend time thinking of its significance for your life. Record the word or phrase below, and reflect on it often, even daily.

SUGGESTIONS FOR PRAYER
PAGE 162

Those who have died remain part of the Church. Include the souls in Purgatory in your daily prayer.

PUTTING FAITH INTO PRACTICE

This week, as a result of reading, reflecting, and responding to Chapter 13, I am inspired to . . .

PART II

THE SACRAMENTS:
THE FAITH CELEBRATED

14 THE CELEBRATION OF THE PASCHAL MYSTERY OF CHRIST

INTRODUCTION TO THE CELEBRATION OF THE
LITURGY IN THE SACRAMENTS
—CCC, NOS. 1076-1209

———— READ • REFLECT • RESPOND ————

MARTIN LOVED LITURGY
PAGES 165-166

How have your sacramental experiences helped you see the invisible presence of God in the visible world?

THE PASCHAL MYSTERY
PAGES 166-168

The Paschal Mystery is Christ's passing from death to new life—the central mystery of all of the Church's liturgy. Think of times in your life when you have experienced the Paschal Mystery. How has this drawn you closer to God?

THE SACRAMENTS
PAGES 168-170

Which one of the sacraments is least familiar to you? What would you like to understand better about that sacrament?

LITURGY AND LIFE
PAGES 175-176

In what ways does the liturgy challenge you to make the world a better place? Why?

FOR DISCUSSION
PAGES 176-177

Read the Discussion Questions in this chapter and use the space below to respond to those for which you have an immediate answer. Later, return to the questions you found more challenging, and invite the Holy Spirit to guide you in responding.

DOCTRINAL STATEMENTS
PAGES 177-178

Read the doctrinal statements for Chapter 14. They will help you to focus on the particular content of the chapter. Record in this journal any insights from reading this summary of the chapter's teaching.

--------- MEDITATE • PRAY • ACT ---------

MEDITATION
PAGES 178-179

Slowly and reflectively read the Meditation for Chapter 14. Select a word or phrase that is especially meaningful, and spend time thinking of its significance for your life. Record the word or phrase below, and reflect on it often, even daily.

SUGGESTIONS FOR PRAYER
PAGE 179

As you conclude, read this chapter's prayer, Psalm 149:1-2, 5-6. Include this psalm and the sentence from St. Augustine in your daily prayer.

PUTTING FAITH INTO PRACTICE

This week, as a result of reading, reflecting, and responding to Chapter 14, I am inspired to . . .

15 BAPTISM: BECOMING A CHRISTIAN

BAPTISM IS THE FIRST OF THE SACRAMENTS OF INITIATION
—CCC, NOS. 1210-1284

READ • REFLECT • RESPOND

A BAPTISMAL WITNESS
PAGES 181-182

John Boyle O'Reilly was a very public baptismal witness through his work as an editor. How have you brought the grace of your Baptism into your workplace? Into your family? Among your friends?

EFFECTS OF BAPTISM
PAGES 192-195

This section highlights five effects of Baptism. How does each effect challenge you in your relationship with God, others, and yourself?

BAPTISM IS A CALL TO HOLINESS
PAGES 195-197

We have many ideals of holiness to which we should aspire, including perfection, mercy, and love. What obstacles do you face as you work to live these ideals and strive for holiness?

FOR DISCUSSION
PAGE 197

Read the Discussion Questions in this chapter and use the space below to respond to those for which you have an immediate answer. Later, return to the questions you found more challenging, and invite the Holy Spirit to guide you in responding.

DOCTRINAL STATEMENTS
PAGES 197-198

Read the doctrinal statements for Chapter 15. They will help you to focus on the particular content of the chapter. Record in this journal any insights from reading this summary of the chapter's teaching.

MEDITATE • PRAY • ACT

MEDITATION
PAGES 198

Slowly and reflectively read the Meditation for Chapter 15. Select a word or phrase that is especially meaningful, and spend time thinking of its significance for your life. Record the word or phrase below, and reflect on it often, even daily.

SUGGESTIONS FOR PRAYER
PAGE 199

Read the Prayer for Anointing with Chrism from the *Rite of Baptism*. Include it in your daily reflection.

Record the verse from Colossians (2:12) in this journal and reread it periodically. Record your reactions and insights into the verse.

PUTTING FAITH INTO PRACTICE

This week, as a result of reading, reflecting, and responding to Chapter 15, I am inspired to . . .

16 CONFIRMATION: CONSECRATED FOR MISSION

CONFIRMATION IS THE SECOND
SACRAMENT OF INITIATION
—CCC, NOS. 1285-1321

READ • REFLECT • RESPOND

FRANCES CABRINI, "GO TO AMERICA"
PAGES 201-202

Who is a "Mother Cabrini" in your life—someone who daily responds to the guidance of the Holy Spirit and lives the mission of the Church? How do you imitate that person?

SACRAMENT OF THE HOLY SPIRIT
PAGES 203-204

When have you been aware of the power of the Holy Spirit acting through you? How has that awareness challenged and changed you?

MISSION AND WITNESS OF THE CONFIRMED
PAGES 207-209

The Holy Spirit bestows seven gifts. Which gift do you need to rely on most today? Why?

FOR DISCUSSION
PAGES 209-210

Read the Discussion Questions in this chapter and use the space below to respond to those for which you have an immediate answer. Later, return to the questions you found more challenging, and invite the Holy Spirit to guide you in responding.

DOCTRINAL STATEMENTS
PAGES 210-211

Read the doctrinal statements for Chapter 16. They will help you to focus on the particular content of the chapter. Record in this journal any insights from reading this summary of the chapter's teaching.

MEDITATE • PRAY • ACT

MEDITATION
PAGE 211

Slowly and reflectively read the Meditation for Chapter 16. Select a word or phrase that is especially meaningful, and spend time thinking of its significance for your life. Record the word or phrase below, and reflect on it often, even daily.

SUGGESTIONS FOR PRAYER
PAGE 211

Memorize either the "Come, Holy Ghost" prayer or the prayer from Edwin Hatch, and pray it each morning and throughout the day. Record in this journal how the prayer impacted your day.

PUTTING FAITH INTO PRACTICE

This week, as a result of reading, reflecting, and responding to Chapter 16, I am inspired to . . .

17

THE EUCHARIST: SOURCE AND SUMMIT OF THE CHRISTIAN LIFE

THE HOLY EUCHARIST COMPLETES CHRISTIAN INITIATION
—CCC, NOS. 1322-1419

———— READ • REFLECT • RESPOND ————

AN APOSTLE OF THE EUCHARIST
PAGES 213-214

The Eucharist gave Carlos Manuel Rodriguez strength, joy, and hope. When has the Eucharist given you the grace to live your faith?

THE REVELATION OF THE EUCHARIST
PAGES 215-216

How does Mass help you to connect with Passover, the Last Supper, and/ or Christ's Passion, death, and Resurrection? What makes you aware that Christ is really, truly, and substantially present in the Eucharist?

EUCHARIST TRANSFORMS THE RECIPIENT
PAGES 225-227

How do you offer yourself as a living and spiritual sacrifice at the Eucharist? What stands in the way of making that offering?

FOR DISCUSSION
PAGE 228

Read the Discussion Questions in this chapter and use the space below to respond to those for which you have an immediate answer. Later, return to the questions you found more challenging, and invite the Holy Spirit to guide you in responding.

DOCTRINAL STATEMENTS
PAGES 228-229

Read the doctrinal statements for Chapter 17. They will help you to focus on the particular content of the chapter. Record in this journal any insights from reading this summary of the chapter's teaching.

MEDITATION
PAGES 229-230

Slowly and reflectively read the Meditation for Chapter 17. Select a word or phrase that is especially meaningful, and spend time thinking of its significance for your life. Record the word or phrase below, and reflect on it often, even daily.

SUGGESTIONS FOR PRAYER
PAGE 230

Pray the *Anima Christi* before you begin your reflection on each section of this chapter.

Record any phrases in this journal that deserve additional reflection during the week. Come back to each phrase, and note any insights in this journal.

PUTTING FAITH INTO PRACTICE

This week, as a result of reading, reflecting, and responding to Chapter 17, I am inspired to . . .

18 SACRAMENT OF PENANCE AND RECONCILIATION: GOD IS RICH IN MERCY

IN THIS SACRAMENT OF HEALING WE ARE
RECONCILED TO GOD AND THE CHURCH
—CCC, NOS. 1420-1498

READ • REFLECT • RESPOND

THE SINNER WHO BECAME A SAINT
PAGES 233-234

Like St. Augustine, when have you felt the damaging effects of sin in your life? How has the Sacrament of Penance helped you experience God's mercy and forgiveness?

THE SACRAMENT OF PENANCE
PAGES 237-240

The liturgy of the Sacrament of Penance includes four key actions of the penitent and priest: contrition, confession, absolution, and satisfaction. During these four actions, what is said or done that reveals God's loving and merciful presence to you?

RECOGNIZE SIN—PRAISE GOD'S MERCY
PAGES 242-243

Think of one example from your personal life where you have down-played the reality of your sinfulness. Why has it been difficult to bring this sin to the Sacrament of Reconciliation? How can you prepare yourself to bring this sin to the sacrament?

FOR DISCUSSION
PAGE 244

Read the Discussion Questions in this chapter and use the space below to respond to those for which you have an immediate answer. Later, return to the questions you found more challenging, and invite the Holy Spirit to guide you in responding.

DOCTRINAL STATEMENTS
PAGES 244-245

Read the doctrinal statements for Chapter 18. They will help you to focus on the particular content of the chapter. Record in this journal any insights from reading this summary of the chapter's teaching.

MEDITATE • PRAY • ACT

MEDITATION
PAGES 246-247

Slowly and reflectively read the Meditation for Chapter 18. Select a word or phrase that is especially meaningful, and spend time thinking of its significance for your life. Record the word or phrase below, and reflect on it often, even daily.

SUGGESTIONS FOR PRAYER
PAGE 247

Repeat the Prayer of the Penitent multiple times as you commit it to memory. Use the prayer to clear your mind for reflecting on the chapter. End your reflection time with Psalm 51:12.

PUTTING FAITH INTO PRACTICE

This week, as a result of reading, reflecting, and responding to Chapter 18, I am inspired to . . .

19 ANOINTING THE SICK AND THE DYING

THE SACRAMENT OF ANOINTING OF THE SICK IS THE
SECOND OF THE SACRAMENTS OF HEALING
—CCC, NOS. 1499-1532

──────── READ • REFLECT • RESPOND ────────

I AM AT PEACE
PAGES 249-250

Cardinal Joseph Bernardin is often praised as a model of how to embrace suffering and find new life. How does his example inspire you?

CHRIST'S COMPASSION FOR THE SICK
PAGES 251-252

Imagine that you are one of the people in the Gospel who was healed by Jesus. How did the healing help you better understand God? Do you know anyone who has received the Sacrament of the Anointing of the Sick? How did it help that person?

IMPORTANCE FOR THE COMMUNITY
PAGE 256

What does our culture believe about illness and how to deal with it? In what ways is the communal celebration of the Sacrament of Anointing countercultural?

FOR DISCUSSION
PAGE 257

Read the Discussion Questions in this chapter and use the space below to respond to those for which you have an immediate answer. Later, return to the questions you found more challenging, and invite the Holy Spirit to guide you in responding.

DOCTRINAL STATEMENTS
PAGES 257-258

Read the doctrinal statements for Chapter 19. They will help you to focus on the particular content of the chapter. Record in this journal any insights from reading this summary of the chapter's teaching.

MEDITATION
PAGES 258-259

Slowly and reflectively read the Meditation for Chapter 19. Select a word or phrase that is especially meaningful, and spend time thinking of its significance for your life. Record the word or phrase below, and reflect on it often, even daily.

SUGGESTIONS FOR PRAYER
PAGE 259

Record meaningful words or phrases from the *Pastoral Care of the Sick* selection in this journal. Why are those words or phrases meaningful?

PUTTING FAITH INTO PRACTICE

This week, as a result of reading, reflecting, and responding to Chapter 19, I am inspired to . . .

20 HOLY ORDERS

THE SACRAMENT OF HOLY ORDERS IS AT THE SERVICE
OF THE COMMUNION OF THE CHURCH
—CCC, NOS. 1533-1600

———— READ • REFLECT • RESPOND ————

A SAINTLY BISHOP AND A HOLY PRIEST
PAGES 261-262

Think of one person in your life who has been a model of what it means
to be a priest or bishop. How have you seen Christ acting in and through
that person?

LOOK AT CHRIST, OUR HIGH PRIEST
PAGE 263

In the synagogue, Jesus read a passage from Isaiah 61 that describes Jesus
the High Priest. How does your parish priest continue Jesus' priestly
ministry in your community? How can you better support him?

THE SPIRITUALITY OF THE PRIEST
PAGES 271-272

How is the spiritual journey of a priest a challenge in today's society?

FOR DISCUSSION
PAGES 272-273

Read the Discussion Questions in this chapter and use the space below to respond to those for which you have an immediate answer. Later, return to the questions you found more challenging, and invite the Holy Spirit to guide you in responding.

DOCTRINAL STATEMENTS
PAGES 273-274

Read the doctrinal statements for Chapter 20. They will help you to focus on the particular content of the chapter. Record in this journal any insights from reading this summary of the chapter's teaching.

MEDITATION
PAGES 274-275

Slowly and reflectively read the Meditation for Chapter 20. Select a word or phrase that is especially meaningful, and spend time thinking of its significance for your life. Record the word or phrase below, and reflect on it often, even daily.

SUGGESTIONS FOR PRAYER
PAGE 275

Read the *Placeat* from Priests' Prayers After Mass. Reflect on the gift of humility that is present in the prayer. How can you nurture that gift in the priests you know?

PUTTING FAITH INTO PRACTICE

This week, as a result of reading, reflecting, and responding to Chapter 20, I am inspired to . . .

21 THE SACRAMENT OF MARRIAGE

MARRIAGE IS A SACRAMENT AT THE
SERVICE OF COMMUNION
—CCC, NOS. 1601-1666

―――― READ • REFLECT • RESPOND ――――

GOD'S SERVANT ABOVE ALL
PAGES 277-278

The story of St. Thomas More illustrates some challenges that marriage has always faced and the role of faith in supporting and sustaining marriage. How has faith inspired, supported, and sustained the marriages of Catholics you know?

GOD IS THE AUTHOR OF MARRIAGE
PAGE 279

In the marriages you have seen, how are God's fidelity, tenderness, and love lived out? What helps married people live these ideals daily?

STRENGTHEN MARRIAGE
PAGES 285-287

What married people in your life are witnesses to the power of the total gift of love in marriage? How?

FOR DISCUSSION

PAGES 289-290

Read the Discussion Questions in this chapter and use the space below
to respond to those for which you have an immediate answer. Later,
return to the questions you found more challenging, and invite the Holy
Spirit to guide you in responding.

DOCTRINAL STATEMENTS

PAGE 290

Read the doctrinal statements for Chapter 21. They will help you to
focus on the particular content of the chapter. Record in this journal any
insights from reading this summary of the chapter's teaching.

MEDITATION
PAGES 291-292

Slowly and reflectively read the Meditation for Chapter 21. Select a word or phrase that is especially meaningful, and spend time thinking of its significance for your life. Record the word or phrase below, and reflect on it often, even daily.

SUGGESTIONS FOR PRAYER
PAGE 292

Pray the Blessing of Families. Repeat it regularly during your reflection on this chapter.

Record the phrase from Hosea in this journal. Reflect on it as you read about the Sacrament of Marriage.

PUTTING FAITH INTO PRACTICE

This week, as a result of reading, reflecting, and responding to Chapter 21, I am inspired to . . .

22 SACRAMENTALS AND POPULAR DEVOTIONS

FORMS OF POPULAR PIETY
—CCC, NOS. 1667-1679

——— READ • REFLECT • RESPOND ———

THE ROSARY PRIEST
PAGES 293-295

How do popular devotions like the Rosary give you insight into God's power and his love for you? What other objects, actions, or prayers help you be more aware of God and his presence?

BLESSINGS
PAGE 296

Recall moments in your life when you experienced a blessing, such as a blessing at bedtime by a parent. How did those blessings make you more aware of God's presence in your life?

THE ROSARY
PAGES 298-300

How has praying the Rosary helped you to more deeply understand the Gospel and your response to Christ?

FOR DISCUSSION
PAGE 301

Read the Discussion Questions in this chapter and use the space below to respond to those for which you have an immediate answer. Later, return to the questions you found more challenging, and invite the Holy Spirit to guide you in responding.

DOCTRINAL STATEMENTS
PAGE 302

Read the doctrinal statements for Chapter 22. They will help you to focus on the particular content of the chapter. Record in this journal any insights from reading this summary of the chapter's teaching.

MEDITATE • PRAY • ACT

MEDITATION
PAGES 302-303

Slowly and reflectively read the Meditation for Chapter 22. Select a word or phrase that is especially meaningful, and spend time thinking of its significance for your life. Record the word or phrase below, and reflect on it often, even daily.

SUGGESTIONS FOR PRAYER
PAGE 303

Review the Grace Before Meals and Grace After Meals. Incorporate both Graces in your daily life.

PUTTING FAITH INTO PRACTICE

This week, as a result of reading, reflecting, and responding to Chapter 22, I am inspired to . . .

PART III

CHRISTIAN MORALITY: THE FAITH LIVED

23 LIFE IN CHRIST— PART ONE

THE FOUNDATIONS OF THE CHRISTIAN MORAL LIFE
—CCC, NOS. 1691-2082

———— READ • REFLECT • RESPOND ————

JESUS THE TEACHER
PAGES 307-309

The Beatitudes are the foundation for authentic Christian discipleship and a way for us to attain ultimate happiness. Which Beatitude(s) have you already made a part of your life, and how? Which Beatitude(s) do you find most challenging? Why?

THE RESPONSIBLE PRACTICE OF FREEDOM
PAGES 310-311

As Americans we stand up for the freedom of the individual. At times the exercise of this freedom is at odds with the teaching of the Church. How do you experience and exercise freedom responsibly?

THE UNDERSTANDING OF MORAL ACTS
PAGES 311-312

This section describes the three elements that constitute a morally good act. How can these three elements help you to live as a Christian?

TRUST IN GOD'S MERCY
PAGES 312-313

When have you asked God for his mercy? How does knowing that God's mercy is yours affect you as a child of God?

THE EXCELLENCE OF VIRTUES
PAGES 315-317

Growing in virtue is an important goal. What helps you to achieve that goal? How does being part of the Church help you to grow in virtue?

LOVE, RULES, AND GRACE
PAGE 318

Your conscience is the moral compass that will help you do the right thing. How do you continue to form your conscience as an adult? What teaching in this chapter can help you continue to develop your conscience?

FOR DISCUSSION
PAGE 319

Read the Discussion Questions in this chapter and use the space below to respond to those for which you have an immediate answer. Later, return to the questions you found more challenging, and invite the Holy Spirit to guide you in responding.

DOCTRINAL STATEMENTS
PAGES 319-320

Read the doctrinal statements for Chapter 23. They will help you to focus on the particular content of the chapter. Record in this journal any insights from reading this summary of the chapter's teaching.

MEDITATION
PAGE 321

Slowly and reflectively read the Meditation for Chapter 23. Select a word or phrase that is especially meaningful, and spend time thinking of its significance for your life. Record the word or phrase below, and reflect on it often, even daily.

SUGGESTIONS FOR PRAYER
PAGE 321

Use this passage from the Letter to the Hebrews to pray to the God of peace, asking him to give you a heart of peace and help you to be a catalyst for peace in your home.

PUTTING FAITH INTO PRACTICE

This week, as a result of reading, reflecting, and responding to Chapter 23, I am inspired to . . .

24 LIFE IN CHRIST— PART TWO

THE PRINCIPLES OF THE CHRISTIAN MORAL LIFE
—CCC, NOS. 1691-2082

———— READ • REFLECT • RESPOND ————

A GOD-FEARING, CHRISTIAN GENTLEMAN
PAGES 323-324

Cesar Chavez was guided by the Golden Rule. How do you "do to others whatever you would have them do to you" (Mt 7:12)?

SOLIDARITY AND SOCIAL JUSTICE
PAGES 325-326

Where in your life does prejudice or bias remain? How can you work to eliminate this?

GOD'S LAW AS OUR GUIDE
PAGES 327-328

The Commandments cannot guide us unless we are aware of them. Review the Ten Commandments, provided in the sidebar. How do these Commandments guide your efforts to live a truly Christian life?

THE TEN COMMANDMENTS

1. I am the LORD your God: you shall not have strange gods before me.
2. You shall not take the name of the LORD your God in vain.
3. Remember to keep holy the LORD's day.
4. Honor your father and your mother.
5. You shall not kill.
6. You shall not commit adultery.
7. You shall not steal.
8. You shall not bear false witness against your neighbor.
9. You shall not covet your neighbor's wife.
10. You shall not covet your neighbor's goods.

—Compendium of the Catechism of the Catholic Church, pp. 127-129

GRACE AND JUSTIFICATION
PAGES 328-330

Many people tend to be self-reliant and independent. As we mature we realize that we cannot live a moral life without the assistance of God's grace. Think of a time when you felt weak or vulnerable. How did you become aware of God's grace supporting you?

THE CHURCH AS MOTHER AND TEACHER
PAGES 330-331

In addition to the grace of God, we have been given the Church as our mother and teacher to help us live a moral life. How do you stay informed of the Church teachings that come to you through the pope and the bishops?

FAITH AND HOPE AFTER SEPTEMBER 11
PAGES 332-333

September 11, 2001, was an unforgettable day in American history. How did your faith sustain you at that time? How can faith support you during any crisis?

FOR DISCUSSION
PAGE 335

Read the Discussion Questions in this chapter and use the space below to respond to those for which you have an immediate answer. Later, return to the questions you found more challenging, and invite the Holy Spirit to guide you in responding.

DOCTRINAL STATEMENTS
PAGES 335-337

Read the doctrinal statements for Chapter 24. They will help you to focus on the particular content of the chapter. Record in this journal any insights from reading this summary of the chapter's teaching.

MEDITATE • PRAY • ACT

MEDITATION
PAGES 337-338

Slowly and reflectively read the Meditation for Chapter 24. Select a word or phrase that is especially meaningful, and spend time thinking of its significance for your life. Record the word or phrase below, and reflect on it often, even daily.

SUGGESTIONS FOR PRAYER
PAGE 338

Every day we hear news of wars, violence, and crime. Rarely do we hear good news in the media. This can weaken hope. Pray the Act of Hope at the end of this chapter, reminding yourself that your hope is grounded in God and his promises, not in the things of the world.

PUTTING FAITH INTO PRACTICE

This week, as a result of reading, reflecting, and responding to Chapter 24, I am inspired to . . .

25 THE FIRST COMMANDMENT

"I, THE Lord, AM YOUR GOD. . . . YOU SHALL NOT HAVE
OTHER GODS BESIDES ME" (EX 20:2-3)
—CCC, NOS. 2083-2141

READ • REFLECT • RESPOND

LAY APOSTLE OF THE TWENTIETH CENTURY
PAGES 339-341

Is God central in your life? If so, how do you keep God supreme above all
else? If not, can something from the life of Catherine De Hueck Doherty
inspire you to change?

THE FIRST COMMANDMENT
PAGES 341-343

How does the practice of the Theological Virtues—faith, hope, and
love—help you to obey the First Commandment?

RELATED ISSUES
PAGES 343-346

Recall a time in your life when you did not know the answer to a vital question of faith. How did it feel not to know? How did you find your way to an answer?

THE HOLINESS OF GOD IN DAILY LIFE
PAGES 346-347

How does your belief in God guide the way you live?

FOR DISCUSSION
PAGE 347

Read the Discussion Questions in this chapter and use the space below to respond to those for which you have an immediate answer. Later, return to the questions you found more challenging, and invite the Holy Spirit to guide you in responding.

DOCTRINAL STATEMENTS
PAGES 347-348

Read the doctrinal statements for Chapter 25. They will help you to focus on the particular content of the chapter. Record in this journal any insights from reading this summary of the chapter's teaching.

MEDITATE • PRAY • ACT

MEDITATION
PAGE 348

Slowly and reflectively read the Meditation for Chapter 25. Select a word or phrase that is especially meaningful, and spend time thinking of its significance for your life. Record the word or phrase below, and reflect on it often, even daily.

SUGGESTIONS FOR PRAYER
PAGE 349

The Act of Love, a traditional Catholic prayer, echoes the First Commandment and the Lord's Prayer. Commit this prayer to memory and pray it frequently.

PUTTING FAITH INTO PRACTICE

This week, as a result of reading, reflecting, and responding to Chapter 25, I am inspired to . . .

26 THE SECOND COMMANDMENT

"YOU SHALL NOT TAKE THE NAME OF THE LORD
YOUR GOD IN VAIN" (EX 20:7)
—CCC, NOS. 2142-2167

READ • REFLECT • RESPOND

JOB: THE POOR MAN PRAISES GOD
PAGES 351-353

Think of a time when you experienced suffering. How did this experience cause you to grow closer to God?

THE NAME OF GOD
PAGES 353-356

In a country that celebrates free speech, that freedom is often pushed to the limit. How do you respond to the disrespectful use of God's name in your home or workplace?

HOW GLORIOUS IS YOUR NAME
PAGES 356-357

How can the misuse of God's name around you challenge your ability to remember that God's name is holy?

FOR DISCUSSION
PAGES 357-358

Read the Discussion Questions in this chapter and use the space below to respond to those for which you have an immediate answer. Later, return to the questions you found more challenging, and invite the Holy Spirit to guide you in responding.

DOCTRINAL STATEMENTS
PAGE 358

Read the doctrinal statements for Chapter 26. They will help you to focus on the particular content of the chapter. Record in this journal any insights from reading this summary of the chapter's teaching.

MEDITATE • PRAY • ACT

MEDITATION
PAGES 358-359

Slowly and reflectively read the Meditation for Chapter 26. Select a word or phrase that is especially meaningful, and spend time thinking of its significance for your life. Record the word or phrase below, and reflect on it often, even daily.

SUGGESTIONS FOR PRAYER
PAGE 359

The passage from Psalm 103 concludes, "Bless his holy name!" Recite this silently to yourself every time you hear God's name misused.

PUTTING FAITH INTO PRACTICE

This week, as a result of reading, reflecting, and responding to Chapter 26, I am inspired to . . .

27 THE THIRD COMMANDMENT

REMEMBER TO KEEP HOLY THE Lord's DAY
—CCC, NOS. 2168-2195

READ • REFLECT • RESPOND

IT'S THE MASS THAT MATTERS
PAGES 361-363

Despite many obstacles, Fr. Gallitzin and Fr. Fitton provided the faithful of their day with the opportunity to attend Mass. How do you affirm the priests who make it possible for you to attend Mass regularly?

THE SABBATH DAY
PAGE 363

The scriptural history of the Sabbath reveals it was a day for worshiping God and relaxing with family. How do you and your family make Sunday special? Does your Sunday tradition reflect this scriptural purpose?

THIS IS THE DAY THE LORD HAS MADE
PAGES 364-365

How has your participation in the Eucharist matured?

WHY GO TO CHURCH ON SUNDAY?

PAGES 365-367

Attending Mass on Sunday is the most important act of the week. How do you make Sunday Mass a priority in your life and your family? Can you do more to make it a priority?

RESTORE SUNDAY

PAGES 367-369

So much in our society battles the religious aspect of Sunday. In what ways do you try to maintain Sunday as a day for God and family?

FOR DISCUSSION

PAGE 369

Read the Discussion Questions in this chapter and use the space below to respond to those for which you have an immediate answer. Later, return to the questions you found more challenging, and invite the Holy Spirit to guide you in responding.

DOCTRINAL STATEMENTS
PAGES 369-370

Read the doctrinal statements for Chapter 27. They will help you to focus on the particular content of the chapter. Record in this journal any insights from reading this summary of the chapter's teaching.

MEDITATE • PRAY • ACT

MEDITATION
PAGES 370-371

Slowly and reflectively read the Meditation for Chapter 27. Select a word or phrase that is especially meaningful, and spend time thinking of its significance for your life. Record the word or phrase below, and reflect on it often, even daily.

SUGGESTIONS FOR PRAYER
PAGE 371

Choose one of the first three verses of Psalm 95, at the end of this chapter. Say the verse as a prayer of praise to the Lord, the great God.

PUTTING FAITH INTO PRACTICE

This week, as a result of reading, reflecting, and responding to Chapter 27, I am inspired to . . .

28 THE FOURTH COMMANDMENT

HONOR YOUR FATHER AND YOUR MOTHER
—CCC, NOS. 2196-2257

READ • REFLECT • RESPOND

THE MARRIED AMONG THE BLESSED
PAGES 373-375

How do you relate to the story of Maria and Luigi Quattrochi? What message from their family life would you like your family to hear?

THE CHRISTIAN FAMILY
PAGES 375-376

How can practicing the Fourth Commandment help your family?

THE DOMESTIC CHURCH
PAGES 376-377

Governments and organizations constantly attempt to redefine the family. Do you recognize your family in the descriptions of "family" found in this section? In what way?

CHILDREN'S LOVE FOR THEIR PARENTS
PAGES 377-378

If you have children or work with them, how do you teach them to show love for their parents?

PARENTS' LOVE FOR THEIR CHILDREN
PAGES 378-379

How has your relationship with your parents influenced your ideas on parenting? If you have children, how do you show your love for each of them?

THE FAMILY AND SOCIETY
PAGES 379-380

How active are you in promoting the rights of the family within your parish? Your school? Your workplace? Your community? Your nation?

WITNESS FIDELITY IN MARRIAGE
PAGES 381-382

In what ways does your family take time to be together? How can you improve the quality and quantity of this time?

FOR DISCUSSION
PAGE 382

Read the Discussion Questions in this chapter and use the space below to respond to those for which you have an immediate answer. Later, return to the questions you found more challenging, and invite the Holy Spirit to guide you in responding.

DOCTRINAL STATEMENTS
PAGES 382-383

Read the doctrinal statements for Chapter 28. They will help you to focus on the particular content of the chapter. Record in this journal any insights from reading this summary of the chapter's teaching.

MEDITATE • PRAY • ACT

MEDITATION
PAGES 383-384

Slowly and reflectively read the Meditation for Chapter 28. Select a word or phrase that is especially meaningful, and spend time thinking of its significance for your life. Record the word or phrase below, and reflect on it often, even daily.

SUGGESTIONS FOR PRAYER
PAGE 385

If you have children, letting them see you pray is very important. Pray this Blessing by Parents for Their Children with your family, possibly at the end of a family meal.

PUTTING FAITH INTO PRACTICE

This week, as a result of reading, reflecting, and responding to Chapter 28, I am inspired to . . .

29 THE FIFTH COMMANDMENT

YOU SHALL NOT KILL
—CCC, NOS. 2258-2330

─────── READ • REFLECT • RESPOND ───────

THE DOROTHY DAY STORY
PAGES 387-389

What stands out in the life of Dorothy Day?

RESPECT HUMAN LIFE
PAGES 389-390

This section lists three challenges to upholding the Fifth Commandment. Of these three, which one do you think is the most critical, and why? What can you do to meet that challenge?

LIFE ISSUES THAT CONFRONT US
PAGES 390-400

How does our society promote a culture of life?

How does the Church's teaching on the sacredness of human life inform your opinions?

FOR DISCUSSION
PAGE 400

Read the Discussion Questions in this chapter and use the space below to respond to those for which you have an immediate answer. Later, return to the questions you found more challenging, and invite the Holy Spirit to guide you in responding.

DOCTRINAL STATEMENTS
PAGES 400-401

Read the doctrinal statements for Chapter 29. They will help you to focus on the particular content of the chapter. Record in this journal any insights from reading this summary of the chapter's teaching.

MEDITATION
PAGES 401-402

Slowly and reflectively read the Meditation for Chapter 29. Select a word or phrase that is especially meaningful, and spend time thinking of its significance for your life. Record the word or phrase below, and reflect on it often, even daily.

SUGGESTIONS FOR PRAYER
PAGE 402

This prayer of St. Francis of Assisi is among the most beloved of prayers. Now that you have reflected on life and death issues in this chapter, allow praying this prayer of peace to be a source of consolation.

PUTTING FAITH INTO PRACTICE

This week, as a result of reading, reflecting, and responding to Chapter 29, I am inspired to . . .

30 THE SIXTH COMMANDMENT

YOU SHALL NOT COMMIT ADULTERY
—CCC, NOS. 2331-2400

READ • REFLECT • RESPOND

PRACTICE MARITAL FIDELITY
PAGES 404-405

The Church teaches that sexuality involves the whole person—the unity of the body and the soul. How does this teaching differ from the way in which segments of our society present sexuality?

CHASTITY
PAGES 405-407

This section teaches about chastity and various sins against this virtue. How does a Christian remain chaste in a world in which so many of these sins exist?

THE LOVE OF HUSBAND AND WIFE
PAGES 408-409

God has established an inseparable bond between the unitive love and the procreative aspects of marriage. How do you see these two aspects of marriage forming a single bond between a husband and a wife?

THE LINK OF FERTILITY AND LOVE
PAGES 409-410

Natural family planning (NFP) allows many couples to remain faithful to God's plan for marriage while achieving or spacing pregnancy. How does NFP help strengthen marriages?

THREATS TO MARRIAGE
PAGES 410-411

Today the number of people getting married is in decline. Why do you think this is? What do you think is the greatest threat to marriage?

THE THEOLOGY OF THE BODY
PAGES 412-413

What message does Pope John Paul II's theology of the body have for our world? How can parents use his vision to speak with their children about respecting themselves and others, both spiritually and physically?

FOR DISCUSSION
PAGE 414

Read the Discussion Questions in this chapter and use the space below to respond to those for which you have an immediate answer. Later, return to the questions you found more challenging, and invite the Holy Spirit to guide you in responding.

DOCTRINAL STATEMENTS
PAGES 414-415

Read the doctrinal statements for Chapter 30. They will help you to focus on the particular content of the chapter. Record in this journal any insights from reading this summary of the chapter's teaching.

MEDITATE • PRAY • ACT

MEDITATION
PAGES 415-416

Slowly and reflectively read the Meditation for Chapter 30. Select a word or phrase that is especially meaningful, and spend time thinking of its significance for your life. Record the word or phrase below, and reflect on it often, even daily.

SUGGESTIONS FOR PRAYER
PAGE 416

Let this Nuptial Blessing remind you that the married state is given special dignity through the Sacrament of Matrimony. Today pray for any couples you know who are having marital problems, and ask God to bless and strengthen them.

PUTTING FAITH INTO PRACTICE

This week, as a result of reading, reflecting, and responding to Chapter 30, I am inspired to . . .

31 THE SEVENTH COMMANDMENT

YOU SHALL NOT STEAL
—CCC, NOS. 2401-2463

READ • REFLECT • RESPOND

MOTHER JOSEPH: A FRONTIER NUN
PAGES 417-418

Think of someone today whose attitude toward the poor is similar to that of Mother Joseph. Why does society admire those who serve the needs of the poor? How do you serve those needs?

RESPECT PEOPLE AND THEIR POSSESSIONS
PAGE 419

In your home, workplace, or community, where do you see the Seventh Commandment being practiced? Where do you see this Commandment being abused?

PRACTICE THE CHURCH'S SOCIAL TEACHING
PAGES 420-424

Which of the Church's social teaching themes do you see being observed? How, where, and by whom? Which of these themes do you see being neglected? How, where, and by whom?

THE POOR IN OUR MIDST
PAGES 424-425

How does your parish care for the poor? In which activities of your parish's social action plan do you participate? If you are not already active in this ministry, how can you get involved? Who can you contact about opportunities?

FOR DISCUSSION
PAGE 425

Read the Discussion Questions in this chapter and use the space below to respond to those for which you have an immediate answer. Later, return to the questions you found more challenging, and invite the Holy Spirit to guide you in responding.

DOCTRINAL STATEMENTS
PAGES 426-427

Read the doctrinal statements for Chapter 31. They will help you to focus on the particular content of the chapter. Record in this journal any insights from reading this summary of the chapter's teaching.

MEDITATE • PRAY • ACT

MEDITATION
PAGES 427-428

Slowly and reflectively read the Meditation for Chapter 31. Select a word or phrase that is especially meaningful, and spend time thinking of its significance for your life. Record the word or phrase below, and reflect on it often, even daily.

SUGGESTIONS FOR PRAYER
PAGE 428

Pray, as the prophet Amos did, that justice and goodness may flourish in your home, your parish, your workplace, and our world.

PUTTING FAITH INTO PRACTICE

This week, as a result of reading, reflecting, and responding to Chapter 31, I am inspired to . . .

32 THE EIGHTH COMMANDMENT

YOU SHALL NOT BEAR FALSE WITNESS
AGAINST YOUR NEIGHBOR
—CCC, NOS. 2464-2513

──────── READ • REFLECT • RESPOND ────────

SPEAK THE TRUTH AND LIVE THE TRUTH
PAGE 431

We live in a world where objective truth is denied. Yet as Christians, we possess a body of objective truths: the Ten Commandments, the Beatitudes, the teachings of Christ, the teachings of the Church. How do these truths help you avoid relativism or ambiguity in understanding and living what is right and avoiding what is wrong?

SINS AGAINST TRUTH
PAGES 431-434

How do you live out the truths of your faith in a society that may not agree with your beliefs?

THE RIGHT TO KNOW THE TRUTH
PAGES 434-436

All day we are exposed to news. Often that news is accompanied by the sharing of opinions—it can be difficult to know the "real" truth. How do you navigate these different channels of information to arrive at the truth you need to know in order to form your own opinion?

FOR DISCUSSION
PAGE 436

Read the Discussion Questions in this chapter and use the space below to respond to those for which you have an immediate answer. Later, return to the questions you found more challenging, and invite the Holy Spirit to guide you in responding.

DOCTRINAL STATEMENTS
PAGES 436-437

Read the doctrinal statements for Chapter 32. They will help you to focus on the particular content of the chapter. Record in this journal any insights from reading this summary of the chapter's teaching.

———————— MEDITATE • PRAY • ACT ————————

MEDITATION
PAGES 437-438

Slowly and reflectively read the Meditation for Chapter 32. Select a word or phrase that is especially meaningful, and spend time thinking of its significance for your life. Record the word or phrase below, and reflect on it often, even daily.

SUGGESTIONS FOR PRAYER
PAGE 438

Pray the Blessing of Centers of Social Communication, asking that those responsible for communicating truth do so in a loving and just manner.

PUTTING FAITH INTO PRACTICE

This week, as a result of reading, reflecting, and responding to Chapter 32, I am inspired to . . .

33 THE NINTH COMMANDMENT

YOU SHALL NOT COVET YOUR NEIGHBOR'S WIFE
—CCC, NOS. 2514-2533

READ • REFLECT • RESPOND

MARIA GORETTI: A MODEL OF PURITY
PAGES 439-440

Many lessons can be learned from the story of St. Maria Goretti. Which lesson touched your heart? Why?

THE MORALITY OF THE HEART
PAGE 441

In what ways have prayer and the saving action of the Holy Spirit helped you to resist the world's temptations against the virtue of purity?

MODESTY
PAGES 441-442

A modest person dresses, speaks, and acts in a manner that supports purity and chastity. In what ways do you try to be a modest person?

RECOVERING MODESTY
PAGES 442-444

Immodesty and permissiveness permeate our culture. How does your family deal with these issues? How can you and your family be counter-cultural examples of Christian modesty?

FOR DISCUSSION
PAGE 444

Read the Discussion Questions in this chapter and use the space below to respond to those for which you have an immediate answer. Later, return to the questions you found more challenging, and invite the Holy Spirit to guide you in responding.

DOCTRINAL STATEMENTS
PAGES 444-445

Read the doctrinal statements for Chapter 33. They will help you to focus on the particular content of the chapter. Record in this journal any insights from reading this summary of the chapter's teaching.

———— MEDITATE • PRAY • ACT ————

MEDITATION
PAGES 445-446

Slowly and reflectively read the Meditation for Chapter 33. Select a word or phrase that is especially meaningful, and spend time thinking of its significance for your life. Record the word or phrase below, and reflect on it often, even daily.

SUGGESTIONS FOR PRAYER
PAGE 446

We cannot lead a virtuous life without the grace of the Holy Spirit. Add the Prayer for Purity of Body and Mind to your favorite prayers.

PUTTING FAITH INTO PRACTICE

This week, as a result of reading, reflecting, and responding to Chapter 33, I am inspired to . . .

34 THE TENTH COMMANDMENT

YOU SHALL NOT COVET YOUR NEIGHBOR'S GOODS
—CCC, NOS. 2534-2557

———— READ • REFLECT • RESPOND ————

I WANT TO LIVE AND DIE FOR GOD
PAGES 447-448

The First Commandment calls us to practice the Theological Virtues of faith, hope, and love. Consider the words of Henriette Delille: "I believe in God. I hope in God. I love and I want to live and die for God." How can you make Henriette Delille's words your own?

WHERE YOUR TREASURE IS
PAGES 449-450

As baptized persons, we should counter envy with humility, thanksgiving to God for his gifts, and surrender to the providence of God. What do you find challenging in this statement, and why?

TO BE A CHRISTIAN STEWARD

PAGES 450-454

Living the life of a Christian steward is challenging. What do you find challenging in this section? How can you meet this challenge?

BLESSED IS THE GENEROUS HEART

PAGES 454-455

Reread the previous USCCA section, "To Be a Christian Steward." How can this summary guide you in developing an even more generous heart?

FOR DISCUSSION

PAGE 455

Read the Discussion Questions in this chapter and use the space below to respond to those for which you have an immediate answer. Later, return to the questions you found more challenging, and invite the Holy Spirit to guide you in responding.

DOCTRINAL STATEMENTS
PAGES 455-456

Read the doctrinal statements for Chapter 34. They will help you to focus on the particular content of the chapter. Record in this journal any insights from reading this summary of the chapter's teaching.

———— MEDITATE • PRAY • ACT ————

MEDITATION
PAGE 456

Slowly and reflectively read the Meditation for Chapter 34. Select a word or phrase that is especially meaningful, and spend time thinking of its significance for your life. Record the word or phrase below, and reflect on it often, even daily.

SUGGESTIONS FOR PRAYER
PAGES 456-457

Read this prayer of St. Francis of Assisi slowly and reflectively. Choose a section you particularly like. Sit with it quietly—let it speak to your soul.

PUTTING FAITH INTO PRACTICE

This week, as a result of reading, reflecting, and responding to Chapter 34, I am inspired to . . .

PART IV

PRAYER:
THE FAITH PRAYED

35 GOD CALLS US TO PRAY

THE FOUNDATIONS OF PRAYER
—CCC, NOS. 2558-2758

——— READ • REFLECT • RESPOND ———

THE HOUR THAT MADE HIS DAY
PAGES 461-462

How has your daily prayer cultivated a deeper love for and relationship with Jesus? What challenges make the practice of daily prayer difficult? What supports this practice?

GOD'S UNIVERSAL CALL TO PRAYER
PAGES 463-474

This section describes many sources and manners of prayer. Which best captures and expresses your faith journey and relationship with God today? How can you more regularly incorporate it into your daily life?

"PRAY ALWAYS" (1 THES 5:17)
PAGES 476-477

How does your daily prayer connect you with the Church's liturgy, especially the Eucharist, and help you participate more deeply? How does the Church's liturgy bring you to new insights into your daily prayer?

FOR DISCUSSION
PAGE 478

Read the Discussion Questions in this chapter and use the space below to respond to those for which you have an immediate answer. Later, return to the questions you found more challenging, and invite the Holy Spirit to guide you in responding.

DOCTRINAL STATEMENTS
PAGES 478-479

Read the doctrinal statements for Chapter 35. They will help you to focus on the particular content of the chapter. Record in this journal any insights from reading this summary of the chapter's teaching.

—————— MEDITATE • PRAY • ACT ——————

MEDITATION
PAGES 479-480

Slowly and reflectively read the Meditation for Chapter 35. Select a word or phrase that is especially meaningful, and spend time thinking of its significance for your life. Record the word or phrase below, and reflect on it often, even daily.

SUGGESTIONS FOR PRAYER
PAGE 480

Pray the passages from Psalm 121 or Psalm 42 found at the end of this chapter. In this journal, record the words or phrases that describe your attitude in prayer. How does your understanding of the words or phrases grow and change as you continue your reflection on the chapter?

PUTTING FAITH INTO PRACTICE

This week, as a result of reading, reflecting, and responding to Chapter 35, I am inspired to . . .

36 JESUS TAUGHT US TO PRAY

THE LORD'S PRAYER: OUR FATHER
—CCC, NOS. 2759-2865

———— READ • REFLECT • RESPOND ————

"THIS IS HOW YOU ARE TO PRAY" (MT 6:9)
PAGES 481-483

In the Gospels of Matthew and Luke, Jesus teaches his disciples how to pray. How can you incorporate Jesus' instructions?

THE CENTRAL PRAYER OF SCRIPTURE
PAGES 483-489

Spend one week reflecting on the Our Father. On each day, reflect on one of the seven petitions in sequence, exploring its meaning for you, past and present, and thinking about how that petition challenges you as a faithful believer. Note your reflections in this journal.

PRAY TO BELIEVE, BELIEVE TO PRAY
PAGES 490-492

What Catholic belief are you struggling with? How might you open your heart and bring that struggle to prayer in order to deepen your belief?

FOR DISCUSSION
PAGE 492

Read the Discussion Questions in this chapter and use the space below to respond to those for which you have an immediate answer. Later, return to the questions you found more challenging, and invite the Holy Spirit to guide you in responding.

DOCTRINAL STATEMENTS
PAGES 493-494

Read the doctrinal statements for Chapter 36. They will help you to focus on the particular content of the chapter. Record in this journal any insights from reading this summary of the chapter's teaching.

──────── MEDITATE • PRAY • ACT ────────

MEDITATION
PAGES 494-495

Slowly and reflectively read the Meditation for Chapter 36. Select a word or phrase that is especially meaningful, and spend time thinking of its significance for your life. Record the word or phrase below, and reflect on it often, even daily.

SUGGESTIONS FOR PRAYER
PAGE 495

Begin and end your reflection on this chapter with the Our Father. Each time you pray it, notice which petitions rest most heavily on your heart. Take a few minutes to meditate on those parts of the prayer.

PUTTING FAITH INTO PRACTICE

This week, as a result of reading, reflecting, and responding to Chapter 36, I am inspired to . . .

READ • REFLECT • RESPOND

READ • REFLECT • RESPOND

MEDITATE • PRAY • ACT

READ • REFLECT • RESPOND